the elephant in the corner

poetry

aoife mannix

thetall-lighthouse

for Véronique

with thanks to the following: Apples and Snakes, Ola Animashawun, Geraldine Collinge, Crisis, Michael Donaghy, Zena Edwards, my family, Richard Lewis, Stacy Makishi, Nick Makoha, Patrick Neate, Joan O'Connell, John Paul O'Neill, Malika's Poetry Kitchen, Maja Prausnitz, Cathy Ryan, Heather Tyrrell, Heather Taylor, Angela Williams and Suzy Willson.

a number of the poems in this edition of Aoife Mannix's poetry were previously published in *The Trick of Foreign Words* (2002).

acknowledgements are due to the editors of the following publications in which some of the poems in this collection appeared: *Dead Drunk Dublin, First Time, Foam: e, Global Tapestry Journal, Monkey Kettle, The Book Of Hope, Bolz, X-magazine, Rattapallax, This Is It, Gargoyle, Breathe, KotaPress, tall-lighthouse poetry review.*

Aoife Mannix's work can also be heard on the CD *Did You Forget To Take Your Tablets*, a musical collaboration with Richard Lewis and the CD *voices from the lighthouse*.

cover image by *Laura Robinson*

Published 2005
ISBN 1 904551 13 0
www.tall-lighthouse.co.uk

contents

The day stepped off the shelf
dusted itself down, drew back the curtains,
turned on its heels, laughed
and let out a deep sigh of tomorrow

Summer Holidays

There's something about rain on a roof
that makes me feel small,
as if the years were falling in on me,
and I'm back in the caravan in Ventry

playing snap with myself
because you refuse another round,
telling me patience is a much better game
for bringing the sun back.

The kids from the farm
have a game they love to play,
seeing who can hold on
to the electric fence for the longest.

The cows eye us wearily, I can never remember
whether standing up or sitting down tells the weather,
and then sometimes they do both.

I hate the weird jolt, to the bone, up to the elbow,
and never last long. Those country kids
can hold on forever, their eyes electric.

And they all know how to smoke,
can ride horses, swim in storms,
and head for the big city at the first opportunity.

But leaping from hay bale to hay bale,
sucking straw like cowboys,
the rain drumming on the tin roof,

a beat of every summer,
they seem to have wings
us town kids can only dream of.

Phoenix

You're too busy looking in the mirror
and only feel the shadow of their wings
brushing your hair.

You turn and grab my feathers,
not suspecting they are on fire
or the thick smoke of my breath in your ear.

But you're not listening,
you think I've just turned
the radio up too loud.

You want to rave to chemical violins,
and push the envelope over the edge.
I watch it fluttering down,

a tiny snowflake in the desert,
knowing you haven't bothered
to read the letter inside.

Unwanted Gift

You had a game you loved to play alone as a kid,
turning earth to coffee and serving
the squirrels in acorn cups.

I see you in those old spliced films,
flickering in your bathing suit by a rock pool.
I never knew your hair was blond,
you were the smallest in your class,
liked to dress up as Davy Crockett.

When I bought you the cowboy hat,
I thought I'd ride bareback across
the years I didn't know you,
back to when we didn't speak the same language.
I thought you'd tear open
the wrapping paper of my heart,
and smile your sunshine gap in your teeth smile.

I carried the promise of your surprise
like a warm secret inside my coat all week
but you didn't lasso me with Indian war cries,
your shock was cold, and putting it on your head,
you pronounced it too big,
that it was only a joke anyway,
you'd never wear such a thing.

And it was me who felt like a child
who's the only one in class
not invited to a birthday party.

The night you were born

We went to see Star Wars,
there was a long queue
but we didn't mind

an old man in a small bowler hat
and a tired brown suit
played the harmonica

half dancing,
racing along the crowds
and singing between the bars

our breath hung in the city mist
and the lights of the cinema
smiled on us as we tapped our feet in time.

Just as the doors opened, he flipped his hat over
several times down the length of his arm
and I dropped in a brand new fifty pence piece

he thanked me with a bow
and we were swept into the warm open mouth
of intergalactic battlefields

settling into the popcorn,
I thought of you swimming in inner space
and I knew that evening the force was with us.

Giving up Smoking

The smell from the old cigarette factory
hangs around the school yard, warm and familiar.
Surely I can't be nostalgic about pollution?

But when I see the John Players Wills sign being removed,
and hear there'll be luxury apartments,
I can't help but remember
the first time you offered me a cigarette.

Blowing smoke out the bedroom window
into a night as soft and close as eternity.
In my head you'll always be 1950's black and white.
Cool, dangerous, and a habit I can't seem to break.

Waltzing with my Grandmother

My Nana in her eighties was full of arthritis
and how the world was going downhill,
yet spent three hours on her broken knees
using her locked wrists
to unscrew the plumbing under her sink
to retrieve the wedding ring
that had slipped down the plug hole
while she was doing the dishes,
my Granddad being nearly twelve years dead.

But this was nothing compared to how
when she was young, she used to
lie in bed in her ball gown
so her father would think she was sleeping
and, as soon as his light was off,
shimmy down the drainpipes to run off laughing
to meet my Granddad on the corner to go dancing.
And in one evening, she loved to say,
they would cover miles and miles together
spinning around the hall.

I'm sitting on her leather pouf near her feet
with my coffee going cold
and putting the ashtray under her cigarette just in time
to catch the long finger of ash falling down.
She smoked her fags to the bone.
She tells me how the day after his funeral
she was on the bus into town
and it struck her there and then
that she would never dance again.

But as the evening draws in
she forgets to put the lights on,
our faces are shadows thrown by the fire,
her words burn and swirl
like silk on polished floors
and we both fox-trot into the past.

Listening to Jazz

Nights my Dad was away
and my mother couldn't sleep,
she'd ask me to get in with her.

I loved the huge green eiderdown,
like being warm and safe in a ship at sea.

The wallpaper jungle animals
who danced in the shadow of the bedside lamp.

The sheets so clean and crisp up to my nose
to ward off the arctic cold.

In her drowsiness my mother
would answer questions
she never had time for during the day.

What life was like before television,
how it would be to walk on the moon,
and whether God existed.

Best of all was the way she kept the radio on
and the man with the slow saxophone voice
would take us away on the night train to New Orleans

and further.

Starved

It was your star sign and it killed you.
There are easier ways to learn things you said.
Of course there are.
Sitting at my brother's window looking out
through the curtains with white clouds
drifting down them.
I trace the patterns in the heavens.
The animals wink at me.
I believed that I was not alone, that light
could eat itself for breakfast, lunch and dinner.
Suck the Milky Way through a straw.
You couldn't get enough sugar.

He told me I was no good as a substitute mother.
The spaghetti sauce splashing on the table.
I knew he didn't know how right he was.
I make the phone calls mechanically.
One rented room after another.
No room at the inn. No hospital beds.
The car window smashed.
He said he couldn't understand
breaking things for the fun of it.
But I could. Is anger genetic?
A deep rich seam of lost fathers and black holes.

Opening the fridge and asking what there is to eat.
What is behind the ends of the universe?
The great dinner party in the sky.
You'll eat what's on your plate.
The clock folding in on itself.
Cutting the pieces smaller and smaller.
Hidden in the Brussels sprouts,
the pointlessness of all this nutrition.
Wandering up and down the aisle
to music with the words removed.
The elevator tinkle of lost space travellers.
A trip to the supermarket on the moon.

Can you tell this isn't real meat?
The soya protein of another light year.
Time frozen or canned.
Not allowed to leave the house
without dinner inside you.
I ate the sky and it was delicious. Popsicles
in the heart of winter. I forget their names now.
The constellations I thought were edible.
Loneliness is just another hunger.
That you of all people should starve to death.
There are easier ways. Of course there are.

Christmas Eve

We used to go to the pub to give our presents,
but now there are babies and husbands,
so we go to your place instead.

The answering machine still only has your name,
you say you love him
but sometimes you wish you had your own room.

He talks about companionship,
pregnancy,
how the years settle like snow.

I unwrap your butterfly emeralds,
the miniature cowboy hat.

I always buy things too small.
I don't even own salad tongs.

You still dream of horses.

The wrapping paper flashes joy,
for a moment we are children again.

I arrive too early, sit on the inside of outside,
stare at the photos of weddings, christenings.

You pour more wine,
where has all the space gone?

You insist on giving me a mince pie
for the journey home, so close and so far,
a bridge over tradition, our lives in boxes,
yet still the warmth of surprise.

A Promise

It was that kind of perfect afternoon
they only have in America, years ago,
with the sunshine so hot you could drink it,
and the trees big and green and lush.

You sat on the swing,
your legs too short to touch the ground.
It was a yellow swing and you wore yellow shorts,
a Superman t-shirt, and you were singing
these are the things we can do without and clapping.

I wished you would hold on tighter
as I placed my hand in the small of your back
and pushed, you wanted to go higher and higher,
but I just kept it steady, marvelling
at your absolute lack of fear, your total conviction
that nothing could break our rhythm.

It seemed to me your trust was the one true thing
I could call my own, and I promised you there,
without a cloud in the sky,
that I'd never let anything bad happen to you.

A small boy on a swing on a summer's day.
It came back to me when I had to tell you
she had died, and the way your face collapsed
as if I had pushed you clear out into nothingness.

Your Father, My Father

Your Dad looks the same as in the photograph,
only his hair is a different colour,
grey and less romantic, the hairbrush still in his hand.
He seems tired waiting for the night shift
and remembers the Jack Kerouac tattoo
as being on her ass, wishful thinking,
it was just below her belly button.
Trapped in the sixties, he never did go on the road,
lived with his mother and drank himself to death.
The windows cracked and half boarded up
in defiance of the rising price of property,
takes one alcoholic to know one.

There are motorcycles in the music,
going back to the roots just around the corner.
Your Dad took us to see Raiders of the Lost Ark,
I remember the guy's flesh peeled off
and his eyes exploded at the end.
My mother always liked your father
and he came to her funeral.
She said some people get caught in time and space
and never get over being left for a younger man.

My Dad says he doesn't want to let go,
memories burning him alive but still it's heat.
Asking me which shirt to wear, cool but casual,
going to a party just down the street,
a woman whose name he never mentions.
Not ready yet, his grief deeper than the ocean.
Food on the table, a roof over our heads, but
somehow absent, a shadow that haunts the mountains.
If he slips, one false move, and breaks a leg up there,
exposed alone, he won't make it back to us.
I try to tell him nothing ventured, nothing gained,
and want somehow to make him less lonely,
yet never even thought of inviting him.

They were once drunk in a taxi together,
your Dad and mine,
embarrassing us falling out the door,
and going on about how proud they were
to have such daughters,
two bedraggled King Lears' struggling for their keys.
I tell my Dad he can ring me any time,
but he doesn't, not wanting to be a burden.
My mother was always saying,
you know your father is a good man,
and I never understood what she meant,
until I saw him holding her hand for hours
by the hospital bed.

I used to bump into your Dad sometimes
on late night buses,
before he gave up the booze
and took up AA as a religion.
My Dad says if there is a God,
he doesn't like him very much,
and needs to go easier on the drink.
But we say nothing and it seems the wisest choice.

In the Hospice

I walk through the picture,
the green grass of ghosts,
the overgrown path.
We climb the broken staircase,
the murals peeled away,
the magic of a rusty swing,
the fragments of flowers.
I understand now that
colour is as vital as breathing.

The doctors move in and out
in an endless stream of white.
At night there is a quiet
only the dying can know.
Something beyond vanity,
a quality of light,
a glass shattered,
the wildness of paint,
silence engraved
in swirls of red,
a name remembered,
the smallness of eternity.

You tell me to look out the window,
and for the first time ever
we both see the stars growing closer.

Ghost

It's still there, like smoke on an autumn afternoon
long after the leaves have been burned.
It hangs in my clothes and smells of long ago.
A stone in my shoe, something you used to say,
an echo I can nearly hear.

Turning the radio on
the sky burns bluer.
You're never black and white to me
but only slightly out of vision
as if by turning quick enough
I could catch you laughing.

Your footstep on the stair,
my name called, and I blink.
The sun in my eyes,
your shadow on my skin,
and somewhere on the edges
there is missing you.

The Christmas Tree

Every year she bought at least one new decoration,
the angels, Santa's, drummer boys, baubles.
Furious that winter one of the red glass balls,
from the first evergreen, smashed.
Inside was silver and reflective,
the fragments of all those years
we struggled to plant a real tree,
the needles eating into the carpet.

It was the beginning of her defeat
the Christmas we went plastic,
the flat too small the excuse for our tiredness.

Yet that very last time
we had finally learned to be kind to each other.
She couldn't eat the turkey
and went to bed while we played poker.
We knew we were going to lose.
Now we deal in silence, trying to pretend
there are still forests covered in snow,
where the tree we were meant to have
is shaking proudly in the wind
and stretching its green towards an open sky.

Tomboy

I've known always
I was a freak in sheep's clothing
since I found pink
revolting hearts and unicorns
and Care Bears and My Little Ponies

I was a warrior spy
through the solar jungle
of the Spanish Civil war
forced to hand over my true weapon
for music lessons
and hatching at the goal post
digging tunnels in the sand
abandoned in the desert

I was looking for a fight,
set Barbie's hair alight
watching her face melt,
didn't want to wear that dress
but I never killed any spiders
and I never wanted to hurt anyone
really

Listen

the grass is growing
the egg is breaking
the raindrop bursts

just before silence
there is a symphony
of every song ever heard

Colour

The trees bruise red,
I watch them burning in the garden.
An old man challenges another to a walking cane duel,
the sun kisses their wrinkles.

October has never been this warm.
Cycling home I drink the last of the light
splashed upon the sky,
a joy too bright for dawn.

The wind wakes up my skin,
I search for speed, the familiar roads made fresh.
The music flashes under my wheel,
whole songs suspended in the air.

I drink the whirring notes.
A cigarette rolled,
standing on a doorstep surveying the street.
The strangers pass swiftly.

It's been so long since I felt this light.
The words promise new beginnings, a delicate freedom.
Something I've always wanted to say,
a quality of the sky.

Abstract as a painting, blue kisses, green smiles,
the delicate hush of brown earth.
I soar through the late afternoon traffic,
there's so much space inside me, hope in all its colours.

Firefly

In the garden in the heat of summer,
the night as warm as a glove,
we chase fireflies among the trees,
shouting and calling as we run.

I open my hands a crack
to see his electric orange tail,
then throw him high as a shooting star.

You clap your hands with delight,
slivers of moon flickering in the distance,
the humming of crickets, louder and louder.

We move deeper into the shadow, time set free,
the spiders dance their webs across our faces,
and looking up, the sky is in flames.

Snow in Spring

When I close my eyes to sleep
I see snow falling against my lids

against the shutters of a spring day
a barbecue in the garden
the green of the trees
and the laughter of sunshine

the table is set for dinner
it's warm and full
but something pulls at the corner of my mind
some memory that threatens to overflow
runs through my body colder than winter

as fast as I turn to escape it
push it back, bury it in other Christmases
it becomes again your funeral

On Dun Laoighaire Pier

You look like a woman
whose been torn at the seams

cover me in tattoos
drown me in honey

your smile is a little
down at heel

Eat me for brunch
throw me confetti

you taste of carnations
and cool summer rain

you smell like an Eskimo out in the sun
or a cappuccino on a frosty morning

I want to kiss your fingers
put my laughter through your hair

you stand your guard
I race along the pier

you tear too easily
I'll stitch us back together

Stopping for Coffee

There is time for mocha.

Late afternoons in the park stripped of summer,
the sky falling like a promise.

The trees flash their gold,
a final salute to the dreams we shared.

I catch my breath on swallows. The last Concord ever
landed today, all that speed costs too much.

You're back but for how long?
I'm still headed south.

You can't see where I'm bleeding,
the bruises spread over my eyes, till all I kiss is purple.

The words held back,
I retreat into my footsteps.

The path uncurling through the park,
so much beauty hurts me.

Can I find it in me to tell you goodbye?
Sugar sprinkled evenings, you're not good for me.

I check the time again, always too early,
addicted to my disappointment.

You said you wouldn't make the same mistake twice,
then flew through your promises.

I wait over coffee.
These in between times I treasure autumn,

the last season of love.

Not Said

Out of season, out of time,
I sit in the whirl of the fan
watching the yellow birds

build their nest of feathers,
caught on a barbed fence
it's a long way to fall.

I burn my bridges
only to walk across fire,
the flames warm my bones.

You promise eternal sunshine,
but no-one can remember my face.

The mad man chants his bitterness
eating the food I've never tasted.

Caught between worlds
I've long since abandoned the plan.

Home is a word that haunts me,
the place I thought I'd be by now.

We try on names for size, our secret tomorrows,
pretending to be the same,
is it only ourselves we're fooling?

You draw the curtains, I breathe the shadows,
my dragon questions burn flesh,
you don't admit to know me for who I am.

Back Door Key

Locked out again,
in-between bits that fall between the cracks.

Sipping silence, stretched out on a picnic blanket,
an angel in a yellow t-shirt.

The chicken still too pink
on the inside.

Next door the kids squeal
under the garden hose.

The barbecue crackles sunshine,
summer creeps under the door.

You never remember
where you left the key.

I count the forget-me-nots.
Later there will be wild strawberries.

There is threat of a storm,
I wrap my arms around you just in case.

World Press Photographs

Faces covered in the ash of snowflakes,
a story unread.

The rivers of questions,
blood that is bought and sold,

suicide over a television.
It's the domestic massacres,

the kerosene scars,
the rituals of prostitution.

These words are held hostage,
they cannot begin to answer

the eyes begging for deliverance.

In the prison camp

one soldier cuts the plastic handcuffs
but leaves the hood in place.

Of course it's not enough,
of course it's disorientating,

of course it's humiliating,
beyond shocking,

the severed head,
such purity of hate.

But still there are small details,
a man with a boy in his arms.

What became of them
in that moment when fear was defeated.

History is an open grave,
but we are more than paper.

Chewing over the News

A man accused of murder
met his victim on the internet,
cut him into pieces and ate him.
His defence was that the deceased
had agreed to be his dinner.

This is followed by a discussion
on whether it should be okay to sell
your kidney or bits of your liver,
to keep out all those organs
from starving Indians
with long thin scars
and children to feed.

Mad cow's disease was
caused by enforced cannibalism,
but if we really want to eat each other,
slice up the parts,
shatter bodies like glass,
take as many as we can with us,
bullet spraying, suicide bombing,
stone throwing, missile cruising.

There's no end to mutual savagery,
technology can never give us friendly fire,
at least admit we're our own worst enemy,
gorging ourselves on destruction.
the blood and bones
of our shared humanity.

Trapped in the Snow

The snow covers us with surprise,
the black ice frozen as the wheels spin,
unable to make it up the hill, we abandon the car
and slip slide our way back.

I eat the flakes and throw laughter
in small merciless balls, there's a certain
champagne purity in the white streets,
a beauty that hides the smallness.

This could be New York, this could be
any Christmas place, cold and true
and not lost in the swirl of petty grudges,
breakfast hatred, muddy edges,
the digging under the skin,
the placing of mines, the threat of poison on the air.

I breathe white smoke and it opens my lungs
to winter possibilities, a frozen moment
floating free from the crazy bustle of rainy nights.

The hush of nature muffles the shouting,
the words that turn to slush,
if we could keep this crystal clarity,
this childish wonder, watching our feet
instead of looking over our shoulder,
there's no place we really need to be.

If we had the time to build a snowman,
if we had the nerve to stay out in the cold,
if we no longer had anything to prove.

In this brightness we're just specks in the distance
and the water melting in my mouth tastes like hope.

Warning Signs

When the only message on your answering machine
is a reminder from yourself to set the video,
and your emails are just virus warnings from people
who otherwise haven't bothered
to get in touch with you for well over a year.

When all your post is bills, and the only text messages
you've got are weather bulletins, when even
your mother seems to have given up calling you
and the fish in the bowl share a greater emotional intimacy
than you and your lover.

When you start to suspect you're becoming invisible,
little by little, fading like ink on old paper,
that's the moment to pack your bags.

Run naked singing through the streets,
get drunk and shout into open doorways,
throw parties and invite strangers you meet on buses,
shave your hair off,
wear purple, go dancing,
draw attention to yourself.

It's not a crime.

Noise

the boy downstairs
is having a row
about benefit
over the phone
he worked less
than so many hours
signed off to go home
has filled in the form
his rent is due
went to see them on Tuesday
his name is spelt
he starts again
all this for the third time

he's on hold now and cursing
his voice is rising with the strain

the phone bangs
rings again
the woman next door is screaming
at her screaming baby
the door bell shrieks
more slamming
shouting someone's name
the boy dials
begins to explain again
he claims he is not getting excited
calls her a bitch
please let them give him the money
I would pay anything for silence

The Swimmer

I am screaming behind a wall of glass.
I close the shutters in my mind,
chinks of fear spill into the room.
I burn underwater,
drowning in words half understood.

I practice stretching my shadow,
it is getting thinner.
My eyes are sealed.
I forget to eat again.
The trick is to be invisible.

I replace the lid of silence.
I am inside the tin
placed back in the cupboard
beside the bread board
and the kitchen knives.
I run my tongue along the edge
testing the sharpness of the night.

I am framed white in the doorway,
a hole burned in the paper sky.
Struck by absence the moon shatters.
I devour pieces of glass
cutting my clothes to shreds.

I dive naked into the black.

Samaritan

You tell me it's about listening,
not pouring the answers,
boiling water on an open wound.
The salt sting of other people's advice
not worth the telephone bill,
cos most people know
what it is that's eating them alive.
They're not stupid,
or at least they got the sense to know they're lost,
and some kinds of loss
got nothing to do with maps,
men in suits handing out directions
like they got a hot-line to Christ himself.

None of those books say anything
about who or how you got to love,
just that you should,
and that's the part that's falling on deaf ears
cos it's easy to stand on your mountain
handing out your multiple choice judgements,
ticking your boxes, labelling people like cabbages.

It's not running round shouting and jumping,
shoving your pre-packaged solutions
down the throats of those who've had to swallow
far more than you will ever know about,
it's sitting at four in the morning in a badly lit room
with a few other volunteers who do this
anonymous, first name, need to know only.

And when you pick up that phone
you just got to take the words as they come,
you can't put them on hold
to call the ambulance, the police,
the next door neighbour.

You have to respect their choices,
just asking the questions that help to tell their story
cos for once, this is not about you,
this is about the end of the line
and we have all been there at some point or other.

And even when they're murderers, abusers,
hang up just to reach for the needle, the glass,
doing to their kids the very things that were done to them.
When you want to scream *why don't you leave that man
that's been knocking you around over twenty years.*

Some doors just aren't so easy to walk out of,
and if you think you got the answer,
you don't understand the question.

There are wheels within wheels,
and if you hold your breath long enough,
and really let their tears, a river
crashing through your ears,
you start to see that underneath suffering,
most of us are trying to make a little bit of goodness
in the face of impossible odds.

And there's a heart beating down the telephone line.
And if there were more of us, just listening,
there wouldn't be so many lying by the side of the road,
while you hurry on by every day of your life
not hearing their cries.

Dragon Slayer

As he conjured up Indian elephants
rampaging under the smoky haze of the kitchen lamp

sucking his Marlboros to stories of when he was a cowboy,
Apache chief, wrestled with dinosaurs.

For a man who didn't believe in reincarnation
he had lived a thousand lives in the eyes of his children,

begging to know about the Russian spies, the cosmonauts,
lion tamers, warriors of Kubla Khan.

He had sunk a pint or two with them all,
the dreamers, weavers, wizards and warlocks.

My mother asking if he ever planned to do the crossword.
She put the kettle on to the hiss of supernovas exploding,

strolls along the wall of China, battles
with trolls and other nameless two-headed monsters.

I wondered how, mornings,
he magicked himself

into a man with paper, dressed up in a tie
and no one would guess he had once slain dragons.

Taboo Animal

The elephant in the corner
that nobody ever spoke about
was an awkward beast.

He did his very best
not to smash the china cups
but he was all fingers and thumbs
and his trunk kept getting caught in the curtains.

He stank to high heaven
of peanuts and forbidden trips to the circus,
his enormous footprints
smudged in the Christmas cake.

He knew better than to blow his own trumpet
but could never quite believe
he'd achieved invisibility,
despite closing his enormous eyes
and folding his four legs under him
in an increasingly awkward, painful position.

He tried to concentrate on shrinking
and never used his ears to fly.

He didn't mind so much being ignored
but it was the way, over Sunday roast,
he would slip in a word
and the silence would kick him in the throat.

The elephant in the corner
was unloved and neglected
and kept his secrets to himself.
But despite all his efforts,
he was getting bigger.
It was only a matter of time
before he squashed
them flat.

And you are

you are coffee
you are warm

you are all the dreams I ever had
your skin is soft as swan's wings

you are a transatlantic flight
you are the sheets newly washed on my bed

you are ice cream
you are pistachio

you are all the missing persons on the milk cartons
your smell is roasted chestnuts in Leicester Square

you are a tangerine at Christmas
you are the car wheels splashing through the rain

you are melted chocolate
you are small

you are all the adventures I'll ever go on
your eyes are windows thrown open in summer

you are sunshine
you are delicious

Karma Settee

The landlord said he'd fix the sofa,
battered and broken and worn
with the springs biting through,
it attempted to swallow you every time you sat in it,
suck you down under the cushions
with the combs and takeaway menus and bits of Rizla,
you felt you would never be able to get up again,
and the dazzling green aquamarine
always made you dizzy
as if you were in a storm at sea.

And I said to him, look,
its banjaxed, finished, kaput,
there's no life left in that useless piece of junk
and the kindest thing would be the knacker's yard.

He replied, but what of people who came after me
who might enjoy being tossed in its 1970's embrace
exploring every possible angle of discomfort and malice,
watching the telly in a kind of corduroy quicksand,
God knows how many tenants have drowned in that couch.

I told him I look forward to the miracle of the resurrection,
he told me he believed in reincarnation,
maybe the sofa will come back next time
as a Habitat leather armchair
in a bachelor's pad in Islington.
There is hope for us all.

My Revolution

In my revolution there will be free ice cream, the old
will become young, trouble will be over
                            before it's begun.

My bombs will be hurled as lemonade,
                            shattering laughter
over walls that have crumbled before they were built.

My bullets will bounce back to where they came from,
leaving no scars, just a trail of jelly beans
that will be the new borders, eaten
before there is any need for visas.

My refugees will party in the street,
dancing their music over the front page
before coming home to balloons and streamers
and suitcases bursting with all they have lost.

My soldiers will wear only their birthday suits
and hand out presents of brand new futures
                            that have no ties.

My politicians will be acrobats that ride horses
bareback and never utter a word.

My followers will always be one step ahead of me,
setting off fireworks in nobody's name.

In my revolution there will be free ice cream.

I will survive

As long as I know how to love,
course it's tacky,
heartbreak is a tacky, messy business
and if you never sat on the edge of a sink,
in a ladies' loo, in some dodgy night club
bawling your eyes out
while your best mates and total strangers
put their arm round you saying
he's a bastard, don't worry about it love
then you haven't lived.

And real friends are the ones
who are still there at four in the morning
holding your hair out of your eyes
as you crouch over the toilet bowl,
puking your guts up
in-between long complicated tales
of Michael or Sean or David
or whatever his name is
whose the reason you haven't bothered
to ring them for the past three months.

And they listen to you
with the patience of all the saints put together
until this song comes on,
when they haul you on to the dance floor,
pouring still more vodka and Red Bull
down your throat, and no matter
how sophisticated you think you are,
you will discover you know all the words
and that maybe you won't slit your wrists
over him after all
because as long as there are glitter balls
and pumping music
and friends to put you comatose into the taxi home
you'll be all right.

Doc Martens

My father telling me
you can't wear
those clown shoes
with a skirt
that's more like a belt anyhow
you look ridiculous
but I pay no mind
cos I'm air cushioned
I got ox blood in my veins
I bounce comfortable into a Friday night
I got steel tipped kisses
I could wander for miles
I was made for kicking
not for the mean pinch
of some tottering stiletto
I got my feet on the ground
my love is laced all the way up
vivid purple stomping
eighteen holes and counting
my step is laughing
no blister worry
trying to be somebody
I ain't

Street Music in Dublin

He looks like your typical drunk,
weaving round to his own inner rhythm,

a sort of swaying quick step shuffle
as the two black musicians
hold the crowd in the palm of their hand.

Reggae in the wild air of a Temple Bar night
with the tourists and the kids lining the steps,

while clubbers trip past under the metal statue
of a palm tree. Even the breeze is musical
as coins fall like rain into the open hat.

We're all surprised when they give the drunk the mic,
hooked up to a stereo for a muffled make believe sound.

Expect some sort of slurred sentimentality,
but his voice is as sober as a bell,
his rhythms pure energy.

The crowd smiles as one, hey he's really good,
then is swept into silence by the sheer rawness of his rap.

A shiver down the spine, love and drugs and Ballymun,
like he'd been inside the soul of the world
and lived to tell the tale.

Someone should sign him to a multi-million pound
record deal, but he just drinks up the applause
and stumbles away.

Going to Galway

I can't remember the last time I was here,
or if I ever was, just a story I learnt to repeat
as the bus sweeps through the countryside.
It's green and it's raining and there are ravens.
I try to understand how the ragged,
yellow patches of gorse are the gold in my teeth,
the straggly hedges and broken walls
the lines on my hand.

The radio plays country & western
in between reading out lists of the dead,
here where people would still know their names.
Small, contained, crackling,
a man interviewed about his disappointment,
the football, the county final,
all the students going home,
one small town after another
till suddenly I'm in a square I recognize.

I was here once with my father,
he took a photograph of his broken heart.
The funeral arrangements,
suddenly, tragically, borne with courage,
ghosts haunt the radio waves,
and I haven't got any flowers.

The afternoon is sunken,
I feel deeply unwelcome with the rain on my face
and nobody listening. Stranger than a stranger,
as the brittle woman sips her resentment.

I wonder what I said wrong.
I'm no shaman, no time traveller,
I nearly missed the flight, and suddenly
I know what I should've realised years ago,
or rather what I've always known
but conveniently forgot, I don't belong here,
never have and never will.

Winter in Ottawa

We built igloos,
put a blanket over the top as a roof
and sat eating snow, trying to grasp
how it would be to melt like this,
to have only the polar bears for company.
Lying down in our snow angels,
the wings a swirl of flakes.
That's where we fired ourselves into the banks,
and you dived out of sight.

I stepped on to the ice,
felt it crack beneath my feet,
fear sliding through my veins, I froze,
not able to go forward,
not able to go back,
but sinking slowly,
you screamed and it woke me.
I threw myself to the shore, my feet
solid lumps of wet, burning pain.

They had to carry me back,
and I caught a chill, spent days
tucked up in bed writing my name
on the window,
peering out at the snow,
so solid, so quiet,
like a language I didn't know,
like I was the very last Eskimo,
and this the coldest town on earth.

The Trip to Hat Tien

Clustered waiting for the morning boat,
a slow hot sun deck on top of the world
as we sail off into murky waters.

Some play dice, some play cards, some talk of home.
We drive into the black clouds, clinging to the rail,
but the rain whips us laughing down the metal stairs,
soaked in seconds, the waves white over the sides,
it passes as torrentially as it arrived.
I brave the wind, pulling my hood up,
the salt sting spray on my tongue.

We arrive still swaying and are packed into tuk tuks,
cutting mountain roads, swerving
the beeping of motorbikes.
Glimpses of jungle markets, then traipsing
through the bacon egg village of backpacker hell.
All this way to drip grease,
packed tight with plastic souvenirs.

The beach hits us like oxygen,
a boat taxi turning out to be a long cool drink of water.
Skimming the waves as we smile at speed,
putting full moon ravers behind us,
to arrive in a shattered bay,
the soft roar of waves as we drag ourselves
on to the shore.

Climb a steep hill to be told it's full, eventually
taking sanctuary in a tree house,
collapsing into noodles and beer
at a wooden table right on the edge of a cliff.
Peering down at palm trees,
sand boulders cut from earth,
the sea churning against a pale blue sky.

As it gets dark, we stumble up the beach,
your shadow on the water,
I sit and watch you in the foam,
this long, long journey to come home.
Your footprint in the sand,
the hammock swaying like a ship,
like a dream hung in the trees.
The green covers everything, vivid and wet,
it croaks and whirrs, strange sounds in the night.
The door blows open, you become
entangled in the mosquito net,
hearing strangers on the path
obsessed with the need for locks.

I blink in the red moonlight, come back to bed,
how can I show you how safe we are?
A thousand miles from everything,
just the crickets and the sea,
a sound older than time, a roaring,
rushing rhythm pulsating in my ears.
My bruises turn into yellow maps,
a lost treasure, sand between my toes,
and peace flowing through my fingertips.

The Famine Road

Out past the rocks, where the river burns into the bone,
and not a soul in all the sky,
just a thin bitter cloak of green,
broken and torn, the raw spring of heather,
and the road itself cut with blood
across a land so wild it howls with ghosts.

This barren track leading nowhere
but the circle of a question mark,
dug by the starving to prove their goodness,
stumbling out from a prison cell.

Reach deep into your charity and see
the thinness of their eyes crawling over the horizon,
another day of dust and dirt, spreading
earth over the skin, the crumbled borders
and the sinking heavens, if God exists
then why is the wind so cruel?

The dampness of their shadows echoes in the stones,
even the rain is ashamed,
as the wolves roar out of their stomachs.
To be poor is the unforgivable crime,
divided into tiny parcels,
arrested for being homeless,
the houses with no chimneys, no windows,
just the smoke of this song drifting over the trees
warning that history is burning.
In the empty places there are still footprints,
still ruins of a language destroyed.
Memory is only words but the land itself
cannot hold these skeletons,
they rattle their accusations, a thin whistle at dawn.

This path is haunted, and there is no peace
for those driven underground.
Suffering marches on, and finds new highways,
but here in the middle of nowhere,
the seeds of grief are sown,
and the harvest will not come this year or next,
it withers in your heart. The connections are buried,
and there but for the grace of chance go I,
empty and silent, overgrown with doubt,
and the weeds cut into their graves,
which remain unknown and forgotten.

Urban Development

In the streets they're still drilling,
the rat tat tat of concrete coffins.

Children sleeping on cement,
the roads weave through their hands.

Abandoned car parks,
vast monuments to folly.

The blind men sing of rice fields,
the deaf men sell t-shirts,
cheap copies of a life they'll never know.

The air is thick with exhausted dreams,
an eternal traffic jam.

The young girls decorate the bars,
fairy lights flashing.

They offer up their smiles to foreigners,
delicate beauty in a sprawling jungle.

And every night the stray dogs grow more hungry.

By the Seaside

Where the blue of the sky meets the blue of the water
in some vast space that slowly,
simply spreads through my fingers
till I'm touching the blueness of blue.

Whole oceans under my fingernails,
a seagull swirls a tiny question mark cut into the evening.

The waves lap their answer,
soft as a lion's roar against the shores of time,
the tiny grains of peace, starfish thrown from a boat.

I hoist the sail, the wind catching me
in the palm of your hand.
The water moves liquid silver, a path through Atlantis.

Whole cities on fire, the flames eat up the forests,
a black twig desert that spreads the apocalypse,
the sun an orange ball behind a mask of grey.

Even the feathers are burning,
a brilliance too bright for flying.
Now the sea bubbles sapphire green,
clear cut as a hidden gem.

I can peer all the way to the bottom.
I was born for water,
tight rope walking along the sea bed,
the yellow buoys mark the days.

Here where the seconds hold their breath,
and there is light sweeping the heavens.

Something of the magic of a day ending,
the sand cool under my feet,
my footprints vanish under the waves
and in my mouth there are pearls.

Halloween in Stockholm

Coming back to where I was born,
a city I have no memory of.
Crossing the bridges arm in arm
you take another photograph in the rain.
The shadows of a medieval mist cling to my eyes.
I had lost my family in a fruit market.
You frame the mountains of pumpkins.
A giant paper ghost hanging above the street of lions,
painted witches and goblins laughing behind glass,
the trick of foreign words instantly translated.

I struggle to remember snow.
A young couple sliding in the ice,
a green pram bouncing on the path,
crashing through the years,
I lie blinded by white, cold and lost.
The blue vastness of the midnight sun.
Surprised by responsibility,
my mother wrapping me tight.
Your fear of car crashes.
Sailing through the air.
My breath of snowflakes.
I had forgotten how to walk,
now my feet dance under water.

I have been here before, a polaroid birth,
instant memory pasted in a book.
All that newly-wed hope,
shotguns fired from a balcony.
Like stepping ten years into the future,
moving forward a generation.
The best part going through customs at the airport.
This is for all your adventures.
They were so young and they knew nothing.
My mother scared because I didn't laugh enough.
Too quiet, too deeply buried in winter.
The past is just another disguise.
I don't recognise myself.

Unanswered

I struggle with the translation
and you don't ring me back.

You worry about the air pollution,
if I'll be able to breathe,
while here I wipe away the dust and wonder
how three months turned into six,
why I'm pleading to go to a place
I never wanted to see in my life?

You pull your dates over your face,
maybe this year, maybe next.
No matter how I try to pin you down
you spin the globe,
all the countries of your curiosity,
and the line is breaking up
so you don't hear
the question I keep asking.

When are you coming home?

Keep Moving

my bones make a hollow sound
a dull thud of words unsaid

I draw back my smile
spiked and unsure

stumbling over love
and grumbling with doubt

I have snapped off so many places
the ground splinters where I step

I am invisible and arrogant
my fear is sarcastic

I don't trust myself
I stroll through the mornings with casual cruelty

the afternoons are unforgiving
there is no home in me

my eyes are maps of shadows
if I stay still one moment I will disappear

The Lincoln Lounge

This bar caught forever some time just after the war,
with the map of the world gathering dust
and the bookshelves sighing
under the weight of too many songs,
the jazz disappointment of skeleton masks.
I prop myself up, sip cocktail dreams,
the design of dresses.

After losing the whole orchestra,
I still believe in Paris, world tours.

Even if I'm waiting for a mirage,
I can see your wings,
the film of your life shot on location.
Of course it's mad, no guarantees,
but rolling this dice, I bet on your eyes,
and I can see us in the sun
with all our impossibilities come true.

Keeping the Accent

The barman makes me repeat my order
three times before he finally understands me.
Heads turn and stare, I can feel my hands sweat
and my throat close over the way it did years ago.
Then he tells me my accent is so cute,
he's going to give me one of the drinks for free.
And all the people at the bar smile at me.
And it doesn't make up for the way
they laughed at me at school,
repeating how I said the word potato
over and over like a needle in my ear,
or Alexis Fortgang dropping a worm in my hair
and telling me to fuck off back to the little hole
in the ground I crawled out of.
But still, now that the way I speak is sweet,
I swallow my bitterness
and try not to think about how opening my mouth
used to feel like a betrayal.
The words sounding out of tune,
a fork dropped on a china plate.
Suddenly it's interesting and cool
and everyone wants to go there.
But I still hide behind my pride,
the way I used to long to talk
like everybody else.

Departures

On the tube from Heathrow
the Indian woman across from me is crying,
her little boy staring out the window at the rain.
I search all my pockets inside and out
for any scrap of tissue to offer in place of goodbye.
I want to hold her hand and say don't cry,
please don't cry, but this is England
where eye contact is forbidden.

The tissue is not used, but somewhat crumpled.

She waves away its ragged imperfection,
its pathetic attempt at comfort. I know
nothing of the aeroplanes in her eyes,
the places left behind,
but I fear you're not coming back,
the way the sun here never seems to shine,
and the airports stretch out
like vast frozen deserts.

Haunted

We come back to find the house empty,
the other tenants fled.
They even took the light bulbs,
this hurts more than the fact they owe you money.

We wander through the scraps of rooms,
the sudden echoing silences.
Don't know what draws us to the attic.
Up there is packed with bric-a-brac,
the scattered remains of lives we'll never know.

Boxes full of books, I borrow a few to read.
You find an old Russian soldier's coat,
a perfect fit, along with the ski mask of a child,
a glove with its tongue pierced.
I ask you what it would say if it could talk?

We shift through the plastic bags,
tattered clothes, magazines,
bits of ribbon, a whole stash of birthday cards.
And I wonder if we too are ghosts now,
only we don't know it yet.

Wishing

We lie smoking and shooting stars
across the Milky Way.
You're a much better shot than me.
You have the smile of someone
who smokes from the back of their hand,
a little rough round the edges.
The moon has had his lip busted
and is as lopsided as you.
We are hung upside down,
two of the first sailors who went too far
and fell off the edge of the earth.

Scenic Photography

I took some photos
wondering how they'll bite me
when they're developed
exposed
for the broken fields and jagged streams
of memory beaten down
smashed on the rocks
the wild cry of seabirds
too small and fast to catch on film
the love we never speak of
out of focus smiles on devastated faces
the light was sunken
but at least it didn't rain
it just hung above us
with the threat of water spilling over

I thought I would drown in those far away cliffs
we could nearly hear the feet slipping in the fog
all sense of direction lost
the questions we set ourselves
the mountains keep their answers to themselves
remembering nothing
but haunting the film
flattened and devoid of perspective
laughing at the idea that they would fit
in such a small frame
shrinking us to a fleeting love affair
a footprint in the bog

Remember the one about love?

My breath is small and clipped,
dragging itself along the fog bitten hill.
My eyes are full of cigarette ash.

You have your own version of me,
it weighs too much.
The walls close in,

they are green and trendy
and the laughter around us
is heavy with smoke.

I may be desperate
but I never asked you for an explanation.
I know a broken arm when I see one.

You grin with pain.
Your funny stories about our love affair don't amuse me.
How would you like to be killed?

I don't drown easily.
You have always wanted to strip me in public.
You invent me again.

The bar is closed,
I twirl my glass.
I don't need your professional opinion.

My words are flying down the road.
They are tall and spread their laughter
on the wind.

Sick and Tired

You're bored of me
and there's no cure for that.

No candlelit dinner, no romantic comedy,
no slow set can stop me shivering
under the weight of your indifference.

No feeding the giraffes,
no cart-wheeling on the moon,

no kissing in chocolate sauce
can make you laugh at my jokes
and there's no cure for that.

Love in Winter

You were afraid of a butterfly.
I manage to chase it into the kitchen,
the panicked whisper of its wings against the light bulb.

Cupping it in my hands,
I feel the feather flutter
of its beauty against my skin.

I open the window thinking out in the fresh air, free
is where butterflies belong, forgetting
it's December and the night is cold and full of wind.

When I open my hand it just sits there,
the purple blue patches on its wings reproach me
like eyes at the bottom of a pool.

It would prefer to smash itself
against the heat of the lamp
than soar off into the darkness.

You are fetching a newspaper to squash it.
I don't understand this urge for destruction, and suddenly
remember there are no butterflies at this time of year.

How did this one come to be in our kitchen
just before Christmas? This fragile splash of colour that has
no hope of survival, born at the wrong time of year.

The next morning is cold, yet sunny
and I wonder what temperature does it take
for a butterfly heart to freeze?

Perspective

In this room with the bedside light glowing
in a hotel in a strange city,
I wait for a phone call.
The distant murmur of traffic is soothing,
like I'm floating in a bubble,
high above the humdrum spaghetti junctions
of ordinary afternoons,
the endless loops and spinning back of roads,
I can't see round the next bend.

These tiny pauses,
where I lick chocolate from my fingers,
and think tomorrow I'll be a better person,
I'll be kinder and stronger and more forgiving.

I'll shuffle time more carefully
and count my lucky stars
to make sure they're all still there.
I'll do all those small things I've been meaning
to do for ages, pay bills, book rooms, make that visit
that's been nibbling at my conscience.

But right now the white neutrality of crisp, clean sheets,
on a bed I didn't make, gives a folded peace.
I still feel a stranger, but not being at home,
it doesn't weigh so much.

I'm a balloon released from a small child's hand,
I'm an astronaut,
I'm an angel on a pin,
I'm ink fresh on a page,
I'm so small I'm invisible.

A streetlight seen from an aeroplane,
a necklace snaking across a foreign land,
I see myself retreating.
Packed inside a suitcase.
I'm travelling cargo without a label,
without a destination.
I'm as light as air and as empty as glass.

My skin flows a river of memory,
but I'm twisting all the letters and setting them on fire.
In the ashes lie my teeth, solid metal lumps of anger.
In my essence there is something harder than diamonds.
I scratch myself open, it's not blood,
it's pure liquid nitrogen, kiss me and see.
I'm an atom that's splitting, a solar system out of orbit.
I'm nothing but right angles, a spinning penny.
When you slap me down, I melt through the table.
I'm a phoenix that sings, a dream that wakes up,
a long way from anywhere, and I'm not sure
I want to come back.

Brighton

you say you've never been
on a roller coaster
the aching climbing fear
the sea splashed carelessly below
the sudden dip into screams
the blurred rush of you holding the bags
waving and smiling at my terror
the childish penny click of your camera
my head turned upside down
your sky being my floor

I walk the inside of the wind
catching your hair
you don't like heights
I could see a million city lights
spread out as a carpet
for us to dance along
you wrap your scarf tighter
I could win you a cotton candy afternoon
the sun in your eyes
I grab you to stop you leaving
the orange clouds burning seagulls
I would never want to scare you
you could melt my wings
an ice cream shared
pretending it's nearly summer
the beaches I am putting in your pocket

you say you don't want to fall

Explorer

I'd like to be small enough
to go rolling, laughing
down your breast

to stroll across the beaches of your stomach

I'd make my home
in the cave
of your belly button

and plan great treks across the wilderness of your heart.

Final Performance

This morning the mountains burn snow sunshine,
a golden haze clings to the balcony.
Silence comes as a shock,
the green whispers of days on the run,
beating the rhythm of words.

Turning right over the bridge,
the polished streets, polished smiles,
slight awkward pauses,
terribly polite in their translations.

Asking what a name means,
a radio emptiness,
trying to drag the questions in,
to put a frame around music,
I turn on my best smile.

A clown, an acrobat,
a circus ringmaster in my own lion show.
I clap my hands in desperation,
slipping in and out of my ID card, dazzling
them with the speed of my costume changes,
firing phone calls from a cannon.

The promise of your voice,
real and sure and warm,
if you were here, you'd laugh too,
but on my own,
the joke's not funny.

I run out of cartwheels,
and am weary of nodding my head,
splitting my skin open,
I step out of the bag,
fresh blood on my shirt.

How interesting,
how different,
how totally and utterly cute.

My heart is Houdini
and for my next trick I'll stop breathing,
walk barefoot over hot coals,
stand on my head,
spin myself like a top,
faster and faster, the colours blur,
I'm knocked out by the punch line.

I lie there bruised and unconscious,
the crowd disperses,
this show has left town
and my stories are empty,
not a dream to my name.
I'm just cheap entertainment,
trying to string a sentence together,
whistle the right tune.

In my bones I know it's time to go home.

Storm Approaching

The rain comes down fine as dust,
we cling to the rails of the boat,
the wind whipping our shirts into sails,
the clouds hang black and orange
on the cutting edge of the mountains.

Our past a white churning path twisting into the horizon.

I want to know if I'm still your favourite birthday present
as the sun slips behind the hill.
I remember light fading
as the market place was sprayed closed,
another year swept overboard.

The world could end tomorrow
but this ship speeds toward shore.

You dive closer to me, there is peace even in this storm.

Muse

You always ask if I've written about you.

When I get up in the mornings and run my bath,
drawing back the curtains in the living room
and peering out at the empty street,
the cars still sleeping and the night
only half pulling back the covers.

When I button up my coat,
hurrying to the tube station,
my breath frosty as I put my ticket
through the machine,
rushing up against the crowd
which is always going the other way.

When I go to the shop to buy my sandwich
and wonder if the other people in the queue
know what it is to think of you
every second of every day.

When I click off the gas fire,
shivering into my side of the bed
and wrap my arms around you,
whispering I love you as good night.

All of that is about you,
even if you think this poem is not.